THE 7 CHARACTER STRENGTHS
OF HIGHLY SUCCESSFUL STUDENTS ™

SOCIAL

ARIE KAPLAN

NEW YORK

Published in 2014 by The Rosen Publishing Group, Inc.
29 East 21st Street, New York, NY 10010

Copyright © 2014 by The Rosen Publishing Group, Inc.

First Edition

Library of Congress Cataloging-in-Publication Data
Kaplan, Arie.
Social intelligence/by Arie Kaplan.
    p. cm.—(The 7 character strengths of highly successful students)
Includes bibliographical references and index.
ISBN 978-1-4488-9552-6 (library binding)—ISBN 978-1-4488-9565-6 (pbk.)—
ISBN 978-1-4488-9566-3 (6-pack)
1. Social intelligence—Juvenile literature. 2. Social skills—Juvenile literature.
3. Social skills in children—Juvenile literature. I. Kaplan, Arie. II. Title.
BF723.S62 K365 2014
302.2—d23

Manufactured in the United States of America

CPSIA Compliance Information: Batch #S13YA: For further information, contact Rosen Publishing, New York, New York, at 1-800-237-9932.

CONTENT

INTRODUCTION

Have you ever seen another person across the room at a party and thought, "I wonder what her deal is?" You go over to talk to her and you find yourself thinking, "She's fascinating!" By the end of the evening, you've made a new friend.

Well, did you know that what you just did was one of the most "human" things you could possibly do? That's because you were exhibiting social intelligence. Social intelligence is the ability to get along well with others and for them to get along well with you. It's often referred to simplistically as "people skills," but it's a bit more complex than that. Social intelligence involves the ability to "read" people. Social intelligence makes you aware of the social dynamics that govern various situations. It helps you to come up with effective strategies that can help you achieve your goals in dealing with others.

It was once thought that people's intelligence could be most accurately measured via a simple number—the IQ score, which stood for "intelligence quotient." According to Professor Howard Gardner of Harvard University,

The more you are able to understand and respect the needs, wants, and feelings of other people, the more successful your interactions will be. If you develop social intelligence, you will also develop a large circle of very good friends.

however, intelligence is "multidimensional." This means that there are many different "key dimensions" — or types — of intelligence that can continue to increase throughout one's life. This potential increase in various kinds of intelligence is influenced by the various experiences, growth opportunities, and challenges one goes through.

One of these "key dimensions" is social intelligence. Gardner's theory has gained much support over the past couple of decades. Many other academics, authors, and medical professionals have embraced the idea of social intelligence.

The concept of social intelligence has changed the way we think about our interactions with one another. We've discovered that—as humans—we're wired to connect. The very design of our brains makes them natural—and very powerful—social networking tools. Whenever we talk to another person, we are instantly drawn into a brain-to-brain link.

The wonderful thing about your level of social intelligence is that it's not set in stone. You can increase it, expand it, enhance it, and sharpen it. And by doing so, you can improve your relationships with your parents, your friends, your peers, your classmates, your coworkers, and your girlfriend or boyfriend. You can literally improve your life.

WHAT IS SOCIAL INTELLIGENCE?

In Daniel Goleman's book *Social Intelligence*, the author relates the story of Layne Habib, whose teenage daughter once called a middle-aged woman "old." Habib had to explain to her daughter why the middle-aged woman didn't want to hear that. Her daughter has Asperger's syndrome, which is a developmental disorder that affects one's ability to socialize and communicate successfully with others. Children who have Asperger's syndrome usually exhibit signs of social awkwardness, the expressing of blunt and unfiltered thoughts, and an obsessive fascination with specific topics.

Because she has Asperger's syndrome, Habib's daughter has little grasp of social cues. On another occasion, she taught her daughter that she should wait for a pause to end a conversation, instead of simply proclaiming, "I feel like leaving now," and abruptly walking off.

These teens are playing a game that helps them develop sportsmanship and cooperation skills as part of a program called PEERS that helps autistic kids build social skills.

Her daughter then understood that sometimes, during a conversation, you have to pretend to be interested in what the other person is saying. As Habib told Goleman about her daughter, "She needs to learn the little white lies to use so as not to hurt another person's feelings."

Habib continually teaches her daughter social strategies like this. She does it in a step-by-step manner, on a case-by-case basis, as new social challenges and situations arise. What she's doing, in the long run, is enhancing her daughter's social intelligence skills. In her professional life, Habib also teaches social skills to special needs children whose challenges are similar to those of her daughter. Mastering these social strategies helps them "join the world," as she puts it.

But don't we all have to learn strategies so that we can "join the world"? Habib's daughter might simply represent an extreme version of the education and training that we all need to develop social intelligence and function socially in the world at large. The way we acquire and practice social intelligence is, in the end, similar in kind (if not in degree) for all of us.

INTERPERSONAL SMARTS

Ever notice how some people are really good at "reading" other people they've just met for the first time? They have enhanced social intelligence skills. At its most basic level, social intelligence is the ability to work well with others. Simply put, it's a knack for understanding people.

Let's say you and your friend Jen have just sat down to lunch in the school cafeteria. A new girl who's just been transferred to your school is nervously scouring the area trying to find a place to sit. Jen motions for the new girl to come over and join you. They start talking, and the new girl's nervousness vanishes.

Feeling empathy for someone who may feel excluded, unwelcome, or awkward can turn a potentially harmful social experience into one that is positive and transformative for all involved. Always choose to be kind and inviting, rather than mean and rejecting.

She's completely at ease. You're dumbfounded; how did Jen do it? It looks like she has established some psychic rapport with this girl! Jen simply shrugs: "I'm good at reading people, that's all." What Jen really means is that she has an awareness of people's stated (and unstated) goals, hopes, fears, wants, and needs.

SOCIAL INTELLIGENCE PLAYED FOR LAUGHS

Because social awkwardness can often be depicted in a way that is comic and entertaining, television and film characters often demonstrate a squirm-inducing social intelligence deficit. Here are some famous fictional characters who are seriously lacking in social intelligence:

- Sheldon on *Big Bang Theory*
- Cleveland Brown Jr. on *The Cleveland Show*
- Dwight Schrute on *The Office*
- Homer Simpson on *The Simpsons*
- Mr. Spock on *Star Trek*
- George Costanza on *Seinfeld*
- Larry David on *Curb Your Enthusiasm*

These characters' lack of social intelligence skills makes them appear quirky and humorous. That's fine for a fictional character. But in real life, a lack of social intelligence is no laughing matter.

SOCIAL INTELLIGENCE: WHO HAS IT?

Who has social intelligence? It's difficult to generalize with any degree of accuracy. But there are indeed certain professions that tend to attract people with a high degree of social intelligence.

Katy Perry revealed her social intelligence and her kindness by making Jodi Dipazza's dreams come true. Jodi *(left)*, who is autistic, accompanied Perry on the piano during Comedy Central's Night of Too Many Stars telethon to benefit for autism programs.

These include salespeople, teachers, clergy, publicists, and team leaders. Some politicians—like Barack Obama, Ronald Reagan, and Bill Clinton—are beloved public figures. All three are examples of people with extremely enhanced social intelligence. Richard Nixon, on the other hand, didn't enjoy making TV appearances. He was known to be socially awkward and introverted. Nixon didn't bother to work on his social intelligence, and he paid the price for it. So we see that one cannot tell whether someone has social intelligence simply based on his or her career choice.

Celebrities who are known for their social intelligence include TV personality Oprah Winfrey, film director Steven Spielberg, and pop star Katy Perry. Celebrities typically exhibit the classic hallmarks of social intelligence. They have a strong need to be liked, but they don't come off as needy. They "mix well" in social situations. They enjoy group functions and activities. They have lots of friends. They're nimble and lively when thrown into social situations, and they like cooperating and collaborating.

THE FLIP SIDE OF SOCIAL INTELLIGENCE: SHYNESS AND SOCIAL ANXIETY

One day when novelist David Guy was sixteen years old, his English teacher asked him to read his composition aloud. Fearful of his classmates taunting him, he succumbed to stage fright and froze up. Stage fright stayed with him throughout his senior year of high school. Nominated for class president, David declined because he was scared that if he won, he'd have to deliver a speech before the entire student body. In both of these cases, David was frightened of ridicule and he surrendered to social anxiety. How could this have been avoided?

THE CONNECTION BETWEEN SOCIAL ANXIETY AND SOCIAL INTELLIGENCE

Reducing your social anxiety can be done in such a way that it actually enhances your social intelligence. This is

Oral presentations and public speaking can fill you with high anxiety, but you are not alone. It makes most people feel uncomfortable and nervous. Try not to let it paralyze you or hold you back from activities you really wish to pursue.

because there's a relationship between social intelligence and social anxiety. Social anxiety is about looking inward too much, and social intelligence is about embracing the world around you. Also, social anxiety is a type of "self-programming." If you are experiencing social anxiety, you've programmed yourself to be wary of social situations. You now need to "reprogram" yourself. That can be done by taking a few simple steps.

Social anxiety can make you feel like you are always entirely alone, especially when surrounded by a sociable crowd of peers.

For one thing, seek out social situations. This will help you to confront your fears head-on, and you'll start to see social situations as normal. And when you are in a social situation, notice the things around you, rather than just focusing on how you feel. Let's say you're at a party. Focus on the pictures on the wall, the snacks on the table, the type of furniture in the room. Then you can ask the other people at the party about those things: "Hey, did you notice the huge flatscreen TV on the wall? How great would it be to watch the Super Bowl on that?!"

Notice that this isn't a question that invites a simple "yes" or "no" answer. Rather, it's a question intended to jump-start a conversation. By asking open-ended questions like this, you'll be inviting other people to join in a conversation. This makes people see you as more open and friendly. Meanwhile, "yes" or "no" questions allow no

YOUR PERSONAL BILL OF RIGHTS

People who are shy usually avoid new experiences and are nervous around new people. Most normal, healthy children are shy to a certain extent. However, childhood shyness usually gives way to adult self-confidence. When it doesn't, there is a risk that shyness will develop into social anxiety.

What can one do to become less shy and more outgoing? Shyness has much to do with low self-esteem, with the feeling that your thoughts and actions don't count for much. The solution, then, is to revise your sense of self-worth. This isn't going to be done all at once; it's a gradual process. Here's a worthwhile activity: write a list, every day, of your "Personal Bill of Rights." For example, you have the right to be heard, the right to ask questions, the right to achieve your goals. On any given day, depending on your specific circumstances, you might write something like, "I have the right to answer a question in math class without getting interrupted by the guy sitting behind me." Or "I have the right to tell the cafeteria lady that she's being rude by snapping at me for no reason."

By making these lists as specific as possible, you'll be able to pinpoint behaviors that you can flag as shy, and you'll see that you did indeed have the right to be less passive, less inhibited, and less nervous in these specific situations. In short, you'll begin to interact much more skillfully and confidently with others. This won't happen overnight, but it will happen.

leeway for lively chatter or spirited debate. They're just answered quickly, and then the conversation dies out.

If you experience social anxiety, you may also be worried about the possibility that the people at the party might see you as somehow weird or tense. You might be thinking, "Why would they care what I think about the huge flatscreen TV?" But that fear comes from the notion that it's abnormal to be a little weird or tense, when in reality, everyone feels a bit weird and tense sometimes. Once you realize this, you'll feel more comfortable just being yourself in social situations, and your social intelligence will increase. Meanwhile, your social anxiety will decrease. Eventually, it may vanish entirely.

SHYNESS AND SOCIAL ANXIETY: WHAT'S THE DIFFERENCE?

Many people confuse social anxiety with shyness, when the reality is that they're two very different things. If you're shy, and you're invited to a party where you don't know anyone, you'll go to the party. At first, you may not want to be there. But after a while, you'll begin to feel relaxed and sociable.

If you suffer from social anxiety, however, and you're invited to the same party, you'll be so consumed with fear that you'll exhibit physical symptoms such as sweating, nausea, heart racing, and dizziness. You'll avoid going to the party as much as humanly possible. As Gina Shaw wrote in an article for WebMD, "In other words, being shy can complicate your life. Having social phobia can stop it in its tracks."

In terms of severity, shyness may sit several notches below social anxiety disorder, but it can still be disruptive to your life. Therefore, if you're prone to social timidity, you should still learn to get a handle on it.

Social anxiety is not mere shyness. It can actually have alarming physical symptoms like sweating, nausea, and a racing heart.

CHAPTER 3

HOW SOCIALLY INTELLIGENT ARE YOU?

When actor Matthew Lillard (*Scream*, *Scooby-Doo*) was going through his preteen years, he was overweight and felt awkward. Then he discovered acting. Suddenly, there was something he was good at. This changed his life. As he told entertainment journalist Lindsay Miller in a

Though now a successful actor, Matthew Lillard (seen here in the film *Scooby-Doo 2: Monsters Unleashed*) once felt extreme social anxiety as a teen who was overweight and out of step with the "cool" crowd.

2012 video interview for the Web site PopSugar, "When you're a thirteen-year-old kid and you're overweight and you have a severe learning disability, you have braces and glasses…you know, when you find something that anyone in the world says, 'Hey you know, you're not bad at that,' it has an incredible impact on a kid." Lillard used acting to connect with other people, to overcome his awkwardness, and to become more socially intelligent.

SOCIALLY TOXIC

Sometimes people with low social intelligence don't ever improve their social intelligence skills because they're unaware that there's a problem. But there is. Not only are they limiting their own potential relationships with others, but they may also be creating a "toxic" environment for those around them. In his book *Social Intelligence: The New Science of Success*, author Karl Albrecht notes that toxic behaviors "cause others to feel devalued, inadequate, angry, frustrated, or guilty." You have no doubt seen this type of person in one of your classes at school. These people have a bad attitude about everything. They're uncooperative with their partners in science lab experiments. They start fights and arguments in class. They steal personal items from other people's lockers and deface school property. Their interactions with other students are unhealthy. Poisonous. Toxic.

But what if you're the person giving off these socially toxic fumes? What if you don't even realize it?

Some people seem to create a toxic environment wherever they go. Be the person who dispels this toxicity with problem solving, peacemaking, and acts of kindness and courage.

Many people who are creating a toxic environment actually don't realize it. They're so caught up in their own problems at home, school, or work that they don't take a moment to look in the mirror and see themselves as other people see them. If they did take the time to reflect on their behaviors and attitudes, they'd become more aware of the negative effect they have on others.

This kind of personal reflection and insight is called self-awareness. Most people are good at heart, and they certainly

MEASURING YOUR SOCIAL INTELLIGENCE

Do you—or someone you know—have problems with social intelligence? Take this quiz to find out:

- Do you frequently (but unintentionally) invade other people's personal space?
- Do people often say you have poor manners?
- Do you try to duck out of social or public speaking situations?
- Are you mocked or taunted by others because of your inability to fit in?
- Do you blurt out whatever pops into your head, no matter how blunt or insensitive, without considering the other person's feelings?
- Do you often seem to antagonize or offend people but aren't sure why?
- Do you not receive many invitations to parties, get-togethers, or outings?
- Do you get into lots of fights and misunderstandings with even your closest friends?
- Do you have trouble making and keeping friends?
- Do you often feel confused or uncomprehending when someone expresses sadness, anger, annoyance, joy, or enthusiuasm?

If you answered "yes" to two or more of these questions, you probably need to work on your social intelligence skills. Rest assured that your skills can improve with a little effort, practice, and desire!

think of themselves as good people. It's only when you have an accurate and honest sense of self-awareness, however, that the "blinders" come off. You then realize, for example, that perhaps it wasn't a great idea to say that insensitive thing to the lunch lady, school bus driver, substitute teacher, or struggling classmate the other day. Having high social intelligence is partially about increasing your self-awareness and carefully monitoring and editing your words, thoughts, behaviors, and attitudes.

Once you've increased your social intelligence skills, you'll find that your behavior will be nurturing and nourishing to those around you, rather than toxic. You will develop and strengthen relationships, and those around you will feel respected, appreciated, and valued. This is because you'll be noticing the effect your actions have on others. As a result, you'll act more friendly, considerate, and cooperative toward them.

SOCIAL PRATFALLS

In comedy, a pratfall is when a comedian falls in a buffoonish way. Think of all the times you've seen Ben Stiller, Adam Sandler, Jack Black, Eddie Murphy, Will Ferrell, or any other comedian trip, slip, or just plain lose their balance. When they slip on a banana peel or slide across a newly waxed floor or tumble down a staircase, that's a pratfall. It's hilarious, but you don't really respect the person doing the pratfall, do you? In fact, you think of that person as a

Part of being socially intelligent is being aware of the needs of those around you. If you see that someone requires peace and quiet to concentrate, keep the noise level down or move your activity to a place where noise is acceptable.

clown, a bumbler. In the movies, that's fine. In real life, not so much. No one wants to be thought of as a clown. There are many social pratfalls that you should avoid. Steering clear of them will help you increase your social intelligence and be more respected by those around you.

You've seen other people commit social pratfalls. Take this situation, for instance: you've stopped your car at the stop sign. Another car pulls up beside you.

There are a group of teens in that car, around your age. And they really like the music they're playing. How do you know this? Because they've cranked up the volume on the car stereo to such an extent that it's blaring incredibly loudly, broadcasting their taste in music to the whole street. That's a social pratfall. Nobody else cares what music the people in that car are listening to. Nobody wants to be subjected to that music, even if it's the greatest music in the world. Nobody asked the people in the car to make it loud enough so that everyone else could hear it. The people in the car are essentially holding everyone else hostage to their wants and needs. This is a social pratfall because the teens in the car aren't treating the human beings around them like human beings. And the essence of social intelligence is showing respect for your fellow human beings.

How about this scenario: you're studying for a test. Your nose is buried in a book. Your brow is furrowed in concentration. A kid in your class saunters over to your desk uninvited and sits himself down. He then leans over the front of your desk as though you have nothing better to do than engage him in conversation. This, too, is a social pratfall. The kid in your class is selfishly imposing his needs and wants on you and ignoring yours. He wants to talk to you. Ordinarily, there's nothing wrong with that. Under normal circumstances, in fact, his actions would be welcomed. But if you're clearly studying, he should respect your need for privacy, quiet, and concentration.

STRIKING A SOCIALLY INTELLIGENT BALANCE

In his book *Social Intelligence*, David Goleman relates the story of three twelve-year-old boys going to play soccer. One is overweight and is ridiculed by the other two. How does he handle this situation? He points out that he may not be that good at soccer, but he's great at art. Then he compliments one of the other kids on his soccer skills. The other two kids have no way of continuing to taunt the third child because he wears his positive attitude like armor. The boy has emotionally disarmed his two tormentors, and they realize their taunts would never have the desired effect. Besides, he's complimented one of them on his soccer prowess.

In this way, the overweight boy has subtly deflated the other two children's taunts through a game of "social chess." By keeping a positive attitude about himself (his art skills) and the other two (their soccer skills), he has outmaneuvered them. He has come off as friendly, charming, and interesting. Suddenly, the other two boys realize that it would be cruel and pointless to taunt him further.

Being bullied, whether physically, verbally, or emotionally, can make you feel isolated and alone. But you are not alone. Seek the help of responsible adults, lean on your true friends, and always take the high road.

After all, he's so likable! This is the essence of social intelligence. If the two boys had persisted in their bullying, they would end up looking worse than they had hoped to make him look with their taunting.

ASSERTIVE OR AGGRESSIVE?

Assertiveness means asking for what you want in an effective manner. It also means making your presence known and standing up for your rights. But don't get assertiveness mixed up with other attitudes and actions that might seem on the surface like assertiveness. This includes aggressive behavior.

What's the difference? Aggressiveness is a negative character trait, and assertiveness is a positive one. For example, someone who ignores other people's irritation is being aggressive but not assertive. Someone who takes over social situations regardless of other people's feelings is being aggressive but not assertive. And someone who just tells people what to do, instead of asking them what they want, is being aggressive but not assertive. An assertive person takes other people's emotions, thoughts, wants, and needs into account even when insisting upon acknowledgement of his or her own. An assertive person displays social intelligence. An aggressive person does not.

THE PERILS OF PASSIVITY

There can be a thin line separating assertiveness and aggressiveness, with selfishness tipping the balance into aggression. Yet there is one negative character trait that is not at all similar to assertiveness. In fact, it is the polar opposite. This is passive behavior. Passive people never make a demand, even a reasonable demand. They simply accept what they're given in life, and therefore they become socially invisible. This is just as bad—if not worse—than aggression because if you're socially invisible, how will you fulfill your life goals? How will you have satisfying relationships if people barely know you exist?

One of the great things about twenty-first-century connectivity is the ample opportunity it affords for telling your friends and family members how much you appreciate and care for them.

Think of social intelligence as occupying a happy medium between passivity and aggressiveness. It combines the gentleness of the former with the confidence and take-charge attitude of the latter.

You may worry that you are too passive in your dealings with people. If you feel that you're not assertive enough, there are things that you can do to hone your "socially intelligent assertiveness" skills. For one thing, when you're communicating with family members and good friends, let them know you care about them. It doesn't matter whether you're at a party, on Facebook, texting, or talking on the phone. The people who matter in your life sometimes want and need to hear that they matter.

STRIKING A SOCIALLY INTELLIGENT BALANCE

MEET-AND-GREET TIPS

Here are some things you can do to appear more relaxed when meeting new people:

- **Think about your tone of voice:** Make sure it isn't too low and whispery or, on the other hand, too loud, abrasive, and off-putting. Talk to them as though it were the most natural thing in the world.

- **Make—and maintain—eye contact:** This conveys respect for the other person and lets them know that you're confident.

- **Smile:** Even if this situation makes you nervous, think about how exciting making a potential new friend is for you on a gut level. Deep down, you can turn that excitement into either nervous energy or positive energy. Which will it be?

- **Visualize a positive outcome:** Stay positive! Think about the best-case scenario: You're making a new friend. Don't bog yourself down with the negatives or the "what if's": what if they reject me? What if they don't want to be associated with me? Thinking that way is no help at all.

HOW TO EASE IN AND EASE UP

What about when you are interacting with people you don't know so well? In that case, it's a good idea to practice some icebreaker phrases to use at school, parties, and other social occasions. An example of an ice-breaker is a sentence that starts out with "Could I trouble you to…?" For example, "Could I trouble you to lend me a pencil?" Or "Could I trouble you to pass

Striking up a conversation in a social setting can seem like a daunting task. But if you zero in on a person's interests and ask conversational questions about those interests, you'll be on your way to a lively and rewarding give-and-take.

me the pretzels?" This way, you're engaging the other person in conversation without being overly demanding or pushy. You're giving off a nice, relaxed vibe, and the other person will appreciate that.

Speaking of relaxed, repeat this one very important word: relax! You may be nervous when meeting new people, but you should try not to let it show physically. This doesn't mean that you should be phony, that you should pretend to be someone you're not. What it does mean is that you should not let the fear of rejection overtake your central nervous system. Meeting new people is something you'll have to do for the rest of your life, so you may as well get used to it now.

SMART STRATEGIES FOR BOOSTING YOUR SOCIAL INTELLIGENCE

Jim Carrey conquered his shyness by simply allowing his true personality to shine out with great exuberance. Let people see and know who you really are, and you will find many friends who like and respect you for it.

When comedian Jim Carrey was growing up in Canada, he was painfully shy and found it difficult to talk to the other children at school. Then one day during freshman year of high school, Carrey discovered that he could deal with his shyness by making the other kids laugh. He quickly became known as the class clown and grew more popular with his fellow students.

Carrey had found his niche, since he would eventually become one of the most popular comedians in film history. But by becoming the class clown, Carrey had also noticed something just as important as discovering his niche. He learned that if you're friendly, charming, and interesting (good traits for any comedian), people will want to talk to you. In other words, he realized how to be more socially intelligent.

THE IMPORTANCE OF EMPATHY

Have you ever felt like you were really good at sympathizing with someone else's feelings? Did you feel like you could tune in to the way that another person sees the world? If the answer is "yes," you can accurately be described as exhibiting empathy. Having empathy means being able to look at life through someone else's eyes. This is central to sharpening your social intelligence skills. The concept of empathy is relatively recent. During the late nineteenth and early twentieth centuries, prominent thinkers began to consider empathy as an important method in understanding other people's mental states.

The term "empathy" suggests an inner mimicking of another person's feelings. People who show empathy toward others are also generally good at communicating their own feelings, needs, and desires in a gentle, nonaggressive, and effective manner. This can help them in all areas: at work, at school, and with friends and family.

COMMUNICATION

How can you be a more socially intelligent communicator at school or work? Basically, there are several things you need to keep in mind. First, you need to realize that much of human interaction takes place via everyday conversations. What you might think of as mindless, silly chatter with friends

Conversation is the basis for every social interaction and every friendship. Be aware of not only what you say but also how you say it. Thoughtful words and a gentle tone will take you very far socially.

could turn out to be very important. The tone and content of simple conversations can have a profound and lasting effect upon your personal, school, and work relationships.

It helps to keep in mind that people are emotional creatures. They have certain things they need and want to get out of a conversation with you. Satisfying, productive, and enjoyable conversations are—to quote author/economist Bryan Caplan—a "double coincidence of wants." This means that if you and I are having a conversation, you have to be interested in what I have to say. But by that same token, I also have to be interested in what you have to say.

More specifically, there are ways to be a better communicator at work, at school, and at home. For one thing, friendliness is key. Whether interacting with your fellow classmates, your siblings, or your coworkers, always assume that the people you're talking to deserve your respect and kindness. Then act accordingly. Look people in the eye while talking to them. Listen to what they have to say. Try to identify and understand their wants and needs, and ask how you can help satisfy them. Remember, it's more important to make and keep friends than it is to always get your way.

EMOTION MANAGEMENT

The teen years can be a time of great emotional fluctuation, volatility, and stress. How can you control, master, and manage your emotions?

To answer that question, consider some of the rules pioneered by the legendary Dale Carnegie, author of *How to Win Friends and Influence People*. Carnegie suggested that you create your own emotions. What he meant was that if you want to be enthusiastic about something, you should act enthusiastic, and you will actually become enthusiastic. It's almost like tricking your brain into a more positive outlook by seeming to fake it at first, until the feeling becomes entirely genuine.

In this way, you can better control your own emotions by envisioning the "you" you want to be and striving to become more like that person. Similarly, Carnegie suggested that if you're stuck in a negative place emotionally, you should shake it off. Start by simply saying to yourself, "I'm not going to be negative anymore." Negativity is a toxic and unhealthy state of mind. Positivity and enthusiasm, on the other hand, are infectious. When you are excited, positive, and joyous, the people around you can't help but be that way as well. You will feed off and reinforce each other's positivity.

Try to remember that people are creatures of emotion, not logic. You've heard of lightning rods, right? It might be helpful to think of people as "emotion rods." They absorb and receive the emotions swirling around outside of them. And these emotions are broadcast by your tone of voice and body language. Over 90 percent of communication is said to be based on voice tonality and body language—whether you're standing rigidly or in a relaxed way, whether you're speaking nervously and haltingly or comfortably. This has a serious effect on how others perceive you, on what they take away from what you tell them, and on the feelings and emotions you generate in them. And this is why it's so important to be in a positive state of mind when interacting with others.

RESPECTING THE SOCIAL CONTRACT

Another part of managing your emotions—and therefore improving your social intelligence skills—is listening.

THE THREE C'S

Many people try to memorize some sort of phrase, mantra, or set of rules or guidelines to help them improve themselves. One such memory device relevant to social intelligence are the "Three C's." What are the Three C's? Complaining, Condemning, and Criticizing, and they should be avoided at all costs. The Three C's will get you stuck in a tailspin of negativity, and you'll be constantly broadcasting and receiving negative emotions. In order to generate a positive flow of emotions between you and others, try practicing the opposite of the Three C's: Accept, Embrace, and Compliment. You've taken your first steps toward a more positive, optimistic worldview.

In other words, rather than talking about your own wants and needs, listen to and respect the wants and needs of those around you.

If the people you're talking to don't reciprocate, however, they're not fulfilling their end of the "social contract." The social contract is at the heart of every personal relationship, whether it's between two siblings, two friends, two romantic partners, two coworkers, or two students. In any of those relationships, there's an unspoken pact that the two people

For any relationship—between friends, romantic partners, siblings, parents and children—to remain strong and successful, both parties must agree to really listen to each other. They must also talk with, not at, each other.

have made: They will listen to you, and in turn, you will listen to them. You will be there for each other, to support, guide, advise, and help one another as true friends do.

If a friend or family member betrays that pact and stops listening to what you are saying, this means that he or she isn't respecting you. Rather than getting angry, try reasoning with the person and calmly ask why he or she isn't listening. Perhaps there's something troubling going on in other person's life, and that person doesn't even realize that he or she is being selfish. You'd be amazed at how many relationship problems can be solved with a calm, reasonable, honest, and evenhanded chat.

PROBLEM SOLVING

Relationship problems will crop up from time to time, even with the closest family members and friends. When they do, you must rely on your social intelligence skills to solve them. Conflict control is often called for at school. Especially during your middle school years, tempers flare, emotional vulnerability is at an all-time high, and feelings get hurt easily. How do you prevent these conflicts from spiraling out of control?

Before we answer that, it's important to understand a concept known as "office politics." What is office politics? It's when a person uses his or her power or influence to get certain perks or advantages that he or she would not ordinarily be entitled to.

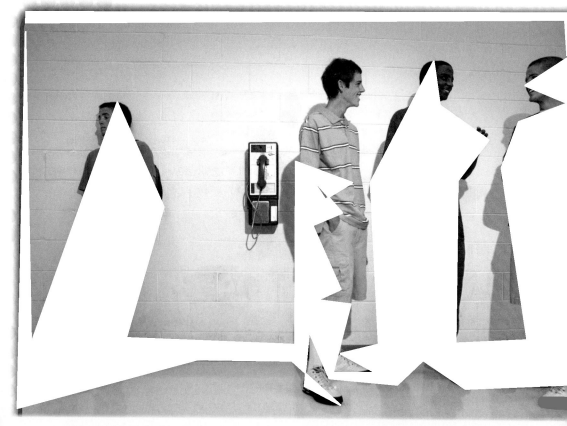

One of the founding principles of cliques is that some people are allowed in, while many others are excluded. It's better to find your own group of like-minded and true friends, rather than wasting a lot of time and effort breaking into a group that doesn't really respect you or allow you to be your genuine self.

The term "office politics" is usually used in reference to the adult world, as it specifically pertains to the workplace. Perhaps you've even heard your parents complaining about office politics at their jobs. However, office politics also exists among your fellow students at school.

For example, there are cliques at every school. A clique is a group of like-minded individuals who exclude people who are deemed to be different from them. Some of the cliques at your school might include the jocks, the cheerleaders, the mathletes, the drama club kids, and so on. Let's say, for the sake of argument, that the school's star basketball player asks if he could cheat off your paper during a math test. He promises that if you let him do so, he will help you become a part of his clique. This is a prime example of office politics at school. In this situation, it is highly unlikely that the basketball player will make good on his promise to help you become a part of his clique. Most likely, what would happen is that you'd get caught helping him cheat, you both would get in trouble, and you'd still be shut out of the clique in question. The payoff, if any, just isn't worth the risk.

There are "politics" everywhere, but this isn't necessarily a bad thing. Often it's a good thing. Just like everyone else, your fellow students crave structure. They like to know that they fit (in some way) within the general structure of the school. But you can solve problems, or even avoid them from developing in the first place, if you use your social intelligence skills to appreciate the wants and needs of your fellow students.

For example, let's go back to the basketball star who asked you if he could cheat off of your test, in exchange for entrée into his clique. In this case, you should politely decline. He might become angry and ask you why you're so uptight. He may ask, "What's the big deal?"

You should tell him, in a calm and relaxed way, that you understand he wants to ace the test. But that if he cheats, it'll be unfair if you did all the work and he got the good grade that resulted from your work. Also, you can tell him that there's no way to ensure you both wouldn't get caught for cheating, and then you'd both fail.

If you tell him this in a cool, measured way, you'll be countering his anger with a reasonable and relaxed approach. Such an approach tends to disarm angry people. He'll have

Social intelligence involves anticipating and appreciating the needs and wants of others. But it is also about being true to yourself. Be the person you want to be, and be the best person you can be. This will allow you to show your true self to others and interact with them with respect and honesty.

no reason to keep talking at you in a loud, angry voice. By talking to him in a calm way, you're implicitly telling him that he's not getting you bent out of shape, so perhaps he shouldn't get bent out of shape either. He'll stop yelling just because he'll feel immature and foolish being the only one getting hysterical. You can also offer to tutor him after school, rather than helping him cheat. This will prove that you've taken his wants and needs into account. You can propose that there is a perfectly acceptable, respectable way to help him ace the test without breaking any rules and getting you both suspended. Of course, it's possible that he'll still be angry and storm off, but at least you tried, and you didn't let him get to you. You showed good social intelligence skills and a mastery of office politics.

Skill in communicating with people of different cliques can also serve you well when dealing with more openly "political" situations in school, such as student govern-ment. If you've been elected to a position in your school's student council, it's very important that you get along with everyone else who's been elected so that you can all work together. Think of it this way; there are more than enough complications and difficulties associated with being a middle school student. Do you really want to add "Have to see treasurer of student council every day— ugh!" to that list? Or would it be better if you're actually friends with the treasurer and look forward to your daily meetings?

HELP

While you should make yourself readily available to help others, think twice before asking people for help. Make sure that this is a problem or challenge you truly can't resolve or fix on your own. You don't want to be one of those people who asks for help with virtually everything he or she undertakes and who comes to rely on outside assistance to fulfill personal responsibilities. If this is a situation that truly requires outside support and perspective, ask for help in a way that makes it easy for people to decline. A good way to ask for help is to say, "How would you feel about...?" A bad way to ask for help is to say, "Please, please just do me this one favor," or "I'm going to need your help with this..."

This is also true if you're part of a club or team at school, such as the yearbook, the cheerleading team, the football team, the drama club, or the math club. Each of these organizations includes many people, each of whom are vital to the success of that group. And everyone wants to know that his or her wants and needs are being met. If you simply let people know that you're listening to them, if you offer constructive ways to help them with their problems, and if you stay optimistic, positive, and constructive in your feedback and attitude, this can only help your relationship with your peers. You can be successful if you understand other people and if you relate to them on a personal level.

THE GREATER GOOD

So far, we've seen what social intelligence could do for you as an individual. We've seen how it can help you maintain a more optimistic and friendly vibe toward your fellow students, your family members, and your coworkers. But what can social intelligence do for the greater good? A growing number of economists now feel that we should work together to build society's capacity for compassion. This means that if people are more compassionate toward one another, it could affect the economy in very positive ways.

How does this work? For one thing, if people incorporate empathy into their everyday lives, they can achieve what Alvin Weinberg, founder of the Institute for Energy Analysis, calls "compassionate capitalism." In a society governed with compassionate capitalism, all citizens are taught to care about the plight of the less fortunate. But you, as a student, need to learn this as early as possible. School curricula should teach social and emotional skills to students. Parents should practice socially intelligent parenting when raising their children. They should show them how to live lives of friendship and positivity, always helping to anticipate the needs and wants of those around them.

The benefits of the compassionate capitalism approach are many. They include higher achievement in schools, better performance at work, more socially well-adjusted children, increased community safety, and healthier citizens. After all, when you've got enhanced social intelligence skills, you're happier, more positive, and less stressed. And when you're in a less stressed emotional state, your mind is healthier, as is your body. Studies show that more educated, healthier, safer, and happier people contribute the most to an economy. So if the majority of Americans have enhanced social intelligence skills, the economy will boom. Stronger, more sustaining social connections will pay instant benefits to everyone. In the meantime, working on your social intelligence skills will achieve the no less desirable and valuable goal of helping you always to be good to yourself and to other people.

GLOSSARY

AGGRESSIVE Pursuing one's goals forcefully, often unnecessarily so; likely to confront or attack.

ANXIETY A feeling of nervousness or unease, especially about something involving an uncertain outcome.

ASSERTIVE Displaying or having a confident, forceful, and positive personality.

AWKWARD Clumsy or inept; lacking in grace, expertise, or skill.

BUFFOONISH Undignified, coarse; like a clown.

DEGREE The level, amount, or extent to which something happens, occurs, or is present.

DUMBFOUNDED To be confused, amazed, or astonished.

DYNAMICS The underlying cause of change or growth; a process of growth, activity, or change. Can also refer to variation and contrast in intensity or force.

ENHANCED To heighten, increase, or improve in value, quality, power, or attractiveness.

GOVERN To exercise continuous control or authority over something or someone.

INTROVERTED Someone whose personality is marked by introversion, meaning that he or she is reserved or shy.

NEUROSIS An emotional and mental disorder that affects only part of one's personality, and which can be accompanied by anxieties, phobias, a mildly distorted perception of reality, and/or other symptoms of psychological distress.

NEUROTIC Someone who is afflicted with a neurosis.

PHOBIC Related to, or suffering from, a phobia, which is an exaggerated fear of a specific object, group of objects, or situation.

PUBLICIST One whose job it is to advertise, or bring to the attention of the public, a product, service, celebrity or public personality, or form of entertainment.

RIDICULE To react toward something with derision or mockery.

QUIRKY Consisting of many peculiar traits or idiosyncrasies.

QUOTIENT The magnitude, or degree, of a specific quality or characteristic.

SELF-ESTEEM Self-satisfaction and confidence.

SUCCUMB To yield to something of superior force, strength, or appeal.

FOR MORE INFORMATION

American Psychological Association (APA)
750 First Street NE
Washington, DC 20002-4242
(800) 374-2721 or (202) 336-5500
Web site: http://www.apa.org
The APA is the largest scientific and professional psycho-
    logical organization in the United States. On its Web site
    are links to various topics and information, including
    dealing with anxiety, bullying, death, and trauma.

Boys & Girls Club
National Headquarters
1275 Peachtree Street NE
Atlanta, GA 30309-3506
(404) 487-5700
Web site: http://www.bgca.org
The Boys & Girls Club provides a safe venue for children
    to grow and learn, as well as a way to foster ongoing
    relationships with caring adult professionals. The orga-
    nization offers programs and experiences designed to
    build character and enhance children's lives.

Center for Creative Leadership (CCL)
One Leadership Place
P.O. Box 26300
Greensboro, NC 27438
(336) 545-2810

Web site: http://www.ccl.org

The CCL focuses on leadership education through its firm belief that strong interpersonal skills, as well as a solid grounding in self-awareness, are the keys to successful leadership.

Girls Leadership Institute

155 Filbert Street, Suite 245

Oakland, CA, 94607

(866) 744-9102

Web site: http://www.girlsleadershipinstitute.org

The Girls Leadership Institute teaches the practices of emotional intelligence and healthy relationships to girls, giving them the confidence and self-esteem needed to be leaders.

Interact

c/o Rotary International

One Rotary Center

1560 Sherman Avenue

Evanston, IL 60201

(866) 976-8279

Web site: http://www.rotary.org

Interact is Rotary International's service club for young people ages twelve to eighteen. Each year, Interact clubs complete at least two community service projects, one of which furthers international understanding and goodwill.

Junior Achievement
One Education Way
Colorado Springs, CO 80906
(719) 540-8000
Web site: http://www.ja.org
Junior Achievement is an organization that educates
students in workforce readiness, entrepreneurship,
and financial literacy through hands-on programs.
Volunteers aim to inspire and empower students to
believe in themselves, to make smart academic and
economic choices, and to make a positive difference in
the world.

Kids Matter
Ste. 401, #151-32500 South Fraser Way
Abbotsford, BC V2T 4W1
Canada
(877) 897-0633
Web site: http://www.kidsmattercanada.com
This organization supports and educates families who
have members suffering from developmental disor-
ders, such as autism, anxiety, ADHD, ADD, and OCD,
that have a negative impact upon their social skills.

Motivate Canada
11 Rosemount Avenue
Ottawa, ON K1Y 4R8

Canada

(613) 789-3333

Web site: http://www.motivatecanada.ca

Motivate Canada specializes in improving the lives of young people by fostering civic engagement, social entrepreneurship, social inclusion, and leadership among youth. The organization uses elements of athletics, physical education, and community-driven development in its programming.

National Youth Leadership Council (NYLC)

1667 Snelling Avenue North

St. Paul, MN 55108

(651) 631-3672

Web site: http://www.nylc.org

The NYLC is devoted to helping young people become leaders in their communities via community involvement.

VIA Institute on Character

312 Walnut Street, Suite 3600

Cincinnati, OH 45202

(513) 621-7501

Web site: http://www.viacharacter.org

Using character strengths assessments for youth and adults, VIA focuses on people's strengths and offers tools and resources to enable individuals to reach the maximum potential of their core strengths. These character strengths can then be applied to work, family, and peer relationships and lead to great success in all aspects of one's life.

Youth Service America
1101 15th Street NW, Suite 200
Washington, DC 20005
(202) 296 - 2992
Web site: http://www.ysa.org
Youth Service America is a resource center that partners with thousands of organizations committed to increasing the quality and quantity of volunteer opportunities for young people, ages five to twenty-five, to serve locally, nationally, and globally.

WEB SITES

Due to the changing nature of Internet links, Rosen Publishing has developed an online list of Web sites related to the subject of this book. This site is updated regularly. Please use this link to access this list:

http://www.rosenlinks.com/7CHAR/Social

FOR FURTHER READING

Armstrong, Thomas. *You're Smarter Than You Think: A Kid's Guide to Multiple Intelligences.* Minneapolis, MN: Free Spirit Publishing, 2003.

Biegel, Gina. *The Stress Reduction Workbook for Teens: Mindfulness Skills to Help You Deal with Stress.* Oakland, CA: Instant Help Books, 2009.

Bradberry, Travis, and Jean Greaves. *The Emotional Intelligence Quick Book.* New York, NY: Fireside Books, 2005.

Carter, Carol. *People Smarts for Teens: Becoming Emotionally Intelligent.* Denver, CO: LifeBound, LLC, 2004.

Carter, Carol. *Success in Middle School.* Denver, CO: LifeBound, 2010.

Covey, Stephen R. *The 7 Habits of Highly Effective People.* New York, NY: Free Press, 2004.

Covey, Stephen R. *The 8th Habit: From Effectiveness to Greatness.* New York, NY: Free Press, 2004.

Delisle, James, and Robert Schultz. *If I'm So Smart, Why Aren't the Answers Easy?* Austin, TX: Prufrock Press, 2013.

Homayoun, Ana. *That Crumpled Paper Was Due Last Week: Helping Disorganized and Distracted Boys Succeed in School and Life.* New York, NY: Perigree, 2010.

Klemmer, Brian. *The Compassionate Samurai: Being Extraordinary in an Ordinary World.* Carlsbad, CA: Hay

House, 2009.

Korgeski, Gregory P. *The Complete Idiot's Guide to Enhancing Your Social IQ.* Indianapolis, IN: Alpha Books, 2008.

Lantieri, Linda, and Daniel Goleman. *Building Emotional Intelligence: Techniques to Cultivate Inner Strength in Children.* Boulder, CO: Sounds True, 2008.

Le Roux, Ronel, and Rina de Klerk-Weyer. *Emotional Intelligence: A Workbook for Your Wellbeing.* Cape Town, South Africa: Human & Rousseau, 2008.

Mayfield, Katherine. *The Box of Daughter.* Rockland, ME: Maine Authors Publishing, 2011.

Van Petten, Vanessa. *You're Grounded!: How to Stop Fighting and Make the Teenage Years Easier.* Bloomington, IN: iUniverse, 2007.

BIBLIOGRAPHY

Albrecht, Karl. *Social Intelligence: The New Science of Success.* San Francisco, CA: Jossey-Bass, 2006.

Burell, Clay. "Why 'Academic Excellence' No Longer Cuts It Today." Beyond-School.org, December 15, 2009. Retrieved October 2012 (http://beyond-school.org/2009/12/15/why-academic-excellence-no-longer-cuts-it-today).

Caplan, Bryan. "How I Raised My Social Intelligence." Library of Economics and Liberty, June 17, 2009. Retrieved September 2012 (http://econlog.econlib.org/archives/2009/06/how_i_raised_my.html).

Carnegie, Dale. *How to Win Friends and Influence People.* New York, NY: Simon & Schuster, 1981.

Coles, Robert. *The Moral Intelligence of Children: How to Raise a Moral Child*. New York, NY: Plume, 1998.

Conan, Neal. "Is Social Intelligence More Useful Than IQ?" NPR.org, October 23, 2006. Retrieved September 2012 (http://www.npr.org/templates/story/story.php?storyId=6368484).

Conway, Martin A., and Christopher W. Pleydell-Pearce. "The Construction of Autobiographical Memories in the Self-Memory System." *Psychological Review*, Vol. 107, No. 2, pp. 261–288.

Covey, Stephen R., A. Roger Merrill, and Rebecca A. Merrill. *First Things First.* New York, NY: Fireside Books, 1994.

Dean, Jeremy. "Are You Just Shy or Do You Have a Social Phobia?" PsyBlog, October 10, 2007. Retrieved

September 2007 (http://www.spring.org.uk/2007/10/are -you-just-shy-or-do-you-have-social.php).

Edberg, Henrik. "Dale Carnegie's Top 10 Tips for Improving Your Social Skills." *The Positivity Blog*. Retrieved September 2012 (http://www.positivityblog.com/ index.php/2008/01/17/dale-carnegies-top-10-tips-for-improving-your-social-skills).

Elias, Maurice J., Steven E. Tobias, and Brian S. Friedlander. *Raising Emotionally Intelligent Teenagers: Parenting with Love, Laughter, and Limits*. New York, NY: Harmony Books, 2000.

Goleman, Daniel. *Emotional Intelligence: Why It Can Matter More Than IQ*. New York, NY: Bantam Books, 1995.

Goleman, Daniel. *Social Intelligence: The Revolutionary New Science of Human Relationships*. New York, NY: Bantam Books, 2006.

Goleman, Daniel, and Richard Boyatzis. "Social Intelligence and the Biology of Leadership." *Harvard Business Review*, September 2008. Retrieved August 2012 (http://hbr.org/2008/09/social-intelligence-and-the -biology-of-leadership/ar/1).

Grundy, Kim. "Jim Carrey Ponders *Mr. Popper's Penguins* and Fatherhood." *SheKnowsParenting*, June 8, 2011. Retrieved October 2012 (http://www.sheknows .com/parenting/articles/833077/jim-carrey-ponders -mr-poppers-penguins-and-fatherhood).

Jancelewicz, Chris. "6 Things You Might Not Know About Jim Carrey." *Moviefone Blog*, June 16, 2011. Retrieved October 2012 (http://blog.moviefone.com/2011/06/16/jim-carrey-facts-trivia).

Kidder, Rushworth M. *How Good People Make Tough Choices: Resolving the Dilemmas of Ethical Living.* New York, NY: Fireside, 1995.

Kindlon, Dan. *Too Much of a Good Thing: Raising Children of Character in an Indulgent Age.* New York, NY: Miramax Books, 2001.

Lane, Christopher. "Shyness or Social Anxiety?" *New York Times*, June 11, 2008. Retrieved September 2012 (http://www.nytimes.com/2008/06/11/opinion/11iht-edlane.1.13635801.html).

Maltz, Maxwell. *Psycho-Cybernetics, A New Way to Get More Living Out of Life.* New York, NY: Pocket Books, 1989.

Markham, Laura. "Social Intelligence for Elementary Schoolers." Aha! Parenting.com. Retrieved October 2012 (http://www.ahaparenting.com/parenting-tools/raise-great-kids/socially-intelligent-child/elementary-schoolers).

Miller, Lindsay. "Matthew Lillard Says His Own Awkward Phase Inspired His Directorial Debut." PopSugar, October 18, 2012. Retrieved October 2012 (http://www.popsugar.com/Matthew-Lillard-Interview-Fat-Kid-Rules-World-Video-25490630).

Montag, Christiane, Jürgen Gallinat, and Andreas Heinz. "Theodor Lipps and the Concept of Empathy: 1851– 1914." *American Journal of Psychiatry*, October 1, 2008. Retrieved September 2012 (http://ajp.psychiatryonline .org/article.aspx?articleID=100211).

Putnam, Nicholas. "Kids Called Nerds: Challenge and Hope for Children with Mild Pervasive Developmental Disorders." AspergerSyndrome.org. Retrieved October 2012 (http://www.aspergersyndrome.org/Articles/Kids-Called-Nerds--Challenge-and-Hope-For-Children.aspx).

Riera, Michael. *Staying Connected to Your Teenager: How to Keep Them Talking to You and How to Hear What They're Really Saying.* Cambridge, MA: DaCapo Press, 2003.

Schwartz, David J. *The Magic of Thinking Big.* New York, NY: Fireside Books, 1987.

Stueber, Karsten. "Empathy." *The Stanford Encyclopedia of Philosophy*, 2008. Retrieved September 2012 (http:// plato.stanford.edu/archives/fall2008/entries/empathy).

Tough, Paul. "What If the Secret to Success Is Failure?" *New York Times*, September 14, 2011. Retrieved October 2012 (http://www.nytimes.com/2011/09/18/ magazine/what-if-the-secret-to-success-is-failure. html?_r=3&pagewanted=all&).

Windell, James. *Six Steps to an Emotionally Intelligent Teenager: Teaching Social Skills to Your Teen.* Hoboken, NJ: Wiley Publishing, 1999.

INDEX

ABOUT THE AUTHOR

Arie Kaplan has written numerous books on pop culture, cultural studies, history, and youth culture. He's also the author of *Gratitude*; *Dating and Relationships: Navigating the Social Scene*; and *Blogs: Finding Your Voice, Finding Your Audience*.

PHOTO CREDITS